AN IDEAS INTO ACTION GUIDEBOOK

Developing
Political Savvy

IDEAS INTO ACTION GUIDEBOOKS

Aimed at managers and executives who are concerned with their own and others' development, each guidebook in this series gives specific advice on how to complete a developmental task or solve a leadership problem.

LEAD CONTRIBUTORS	William A. Gentry
	Jean Brittain Leslie
CONTRIBUTORS	Sara N. King
	Kim Leahy
	Harold Scharlatt
	Bertrand Sereno

DIRECTOR OF ASSESSMENTS, TOOLS, AND PUBLICATIONS	Sylvester Taylor
MANAGER, PUBLICATION DEVELOPMENT	Peter Scisco
EDITOR	Stephen Rush
EDITOR	Karen Lewis
DESIGN AND LAYOUT	Joanne Ferguson
COVER DESIGN	Laura J. Gibson
	Chris Wilson, 29 & Company

CCL No. 452
ISBN No. 978-1-60491-122-0

CENTER FOR CREATIVE LEADERSHIP
POST OFFICE BOX 26300
GREENSBORO, NORTH CAROLINA 27438-6300
336-288-7210
WWW.CCL.ORG/PUBLICATIONS

AN IDEAS INTO ACTION GUIDEBOOK

Developing Political Savvy

William A. Gentry and Jean Brittain Leslie

Center for
Creative
Leadership
www.ccl.org

THE IDEAS INTO ACTION GUIDEBOOK SERIES

This series of guidebooks draws on the practical knowledge that the Center for Creative Leadership (CCL®) has generated, since its inception in 1970, through its research and educational activity conducted in partnership with hundreds of thousands of managers and executives. Much of this knowledge is shared—in a way that is distinct from the typical university department, professional association, or consultancy. CCL is not simply a collection of individual experts, although the individual credentials of its staff are impressive; rather it is a community, with its members holding certain principles in common and working together to understand and generate practical responses to today's leadership and organizational challenges.

The purpose of the series is to provide managers with specific advice on how to complete a developmental task or solve a leadership challenge. In doing that, the series carries out CCL's mission to advance the understanding, practice, and development of leadership for the benefit of society worldwide. We think you will find the Ideas Into Action Guidebooks an important addition to your leadership toolkit.

Table of Contents

EXECUTIVE BRIEF

Politics is not good or bad; it's neutral and natural. Politics is not a zero-sum game; being politically savvy does not mean that someone else has to lose for you to win. Politics is not about being false; instead, political savvy is about using your skills, behaviors, and qualities to be effective, and sincerity is vital. The ideas and exercises in this guidebook will help you become a more politically savvy leader and build your capacity to lead effectively in your organization.

Rex and the Political Missteps

Rex was an expert on a promising technological advancement in his industry. His reputation with a competitor's firm got the attention of senior management. They were so excited when they were finally able to hire him, thinking they had a direct line to unspeakable profits. It didn't take long, however, for Rex's lack of political savvy to get noticed.

Rex's political blunders were obvious to everyone—everyone but Rex. From the start, he took every opportunity to remind people that he was the expert. He concentrated on work that fulfilled his own agenda or interested him personally, disregarding other more important projects that would benefit his team or the entire organization. Then whenever senior management was around, he would steal the credit for the work of other members of his team.

He got the reputation of being nice only when he wanted something. He often made commitments and promises to stakeholders with a handshake and a smile, but he never fulfilled those commitments or kept those promises. Fewer and fewer people trusted him. As a result, his ability to collaborate and build a quality network of people diminished day by day.

Rex consistently overestimated his ability and didn't bother to listen or learn from others. He didn't read situations correctly or try to understand the culture of his new organization. He never seemed to tire of telling people that his former employer did things better.

His superiors made several attempts to redirect him, but their attempts failed. The organization eventually let Rex go.

Workplace Politics—A Fact of Life

Rex clearly had a severe lack of political savvy, but he is not alone. Many leaders have room for improvement. Politics in the workplace is a fact of life. How people feel about that fact varies. To some, the ability to think and act politically feels like a "necessary evil." Others would rather refuse to "play the game," but they fear their careers will suffer if they don't.

Many people would describe politics in their organization as coalition building, bullying, making people feel small, favoritism, stealing credit from someone else, or "stabbing someone in the back (or even the front)"—all for one's own self-interest. In these environments, people make their own interpretations of what is right and wrong because there is no clear, understood way of doing things.

Politics is not a zero-sum game.

There are managers, however, who have learned that being politically savvy can lead to desired outcomes in a positive, authentic manner. In general, they have developed high-quality relationships and networks, they know themselves well, and they have a good sense about what is going on around them. They get the resources they and their subordinates or teams need to function effectively. They too see politics around them, where employees experience competing interests, scarce resources, ambiguity in decision making and authority, unclear rules and regulations to govern workplace behavior, and a lack of information. But politics to them is not a zero-sum game where they work the system to their own advantage and to the disadvantage of others. These managers regard workplace politics as neutral. They are effective because they understand others at work and use that knowledge to influence others to act in ways that enhance personal and organizational objectives.

Organizational politics is neither good nor bad. It simply is the air we breathe in organizations. It's your perception of organizational politics that makes it what it is to you. How you view and respond to politics in your organization can have a great bearing on how well you do your job and how you feel about your organization and coworkers. One way to be effective in the inherently political environment of contemporary organizations is to change your way of understanding politics—to become politically savvy. Once you consider, understand, and accept that organizational politics is neutral and a natural part of everyday occurrences in the workplace, you can appropriately build your capacity to lead effectively in that environment. You can be regarded as someone with effective political savvy in your organization, one who can influence and persuade others in a sincere, authentic manner.

Political Savvy Checklist

How politically savvy are you? Put a check by each statement that is true of you. More checks indicate more political savvy.

Mingle strategically.

_____ I have a diverse network of people who have influence and power within my organization.

_____ I position myself in my organization to create and take advantage of any opportunities that come my way through my network.

_____ Others see me as an effective negotiator and deal broker.

_____ I handle conflict well.

_____ I get things done without creating adversarial relationships.

_____ I am diplomatic in negotiating and making my points clear and understood.

_____ I find common ground with those over whom I have no direct authority in making decisions.

_____ I try to understand things from others' points of view.

_____ Others in my organization count on me.

_____ I am dependable.

_____ I respond quickly to requests from my boss.

_____ I put extra energy into making sure my boss's needs are met.

_____ I make sure my work is in alignment with the goals of senior management.

_____ I am mindful of the needs of my team and my direct reports while I keep those above me informed.

Read the situation.

_____ I accurately interpret what is going on in my environment.

_____ I accurately read and understand others—their thoughts and feelings.

_____ I am sensitive to other people's needs and wants.

_____ I understand other people's goals and motivations.

_____ I have an accurate picture of my strengths and weaknesses.

_____ I see myself as others see me.

Determine the appropriate behavior before acting.

_____ I choose my battles wisely so my energy goes where it counts.

_____ I size up situations before deciding how to present an idea to others.

_____ When presenting an idea to others, I think about not only what I say but how I say it.

_____ I show warmth in my interaction with others.

_____ I put people at ease.

_____ I focus on the positive.

_____ I do not become moody or hostile when things are not going my way.

_____ I am calm in the face of trouble at work.

_____ I own the mistakes I make and do not blame others.

Leave them with a good impression.

_____ Others see me as honest, open, and straightforward.

_____ Others see my intentions and motives as true.

_____ Others do not view me as a manipulative or coercive manager.

_____ I have a style that exerts suitable influence over others.

_____ I recognize and adapt my behavior to the situation to get the best outcome or response from people.

Developing Effective Political Savvy

In some organizations it may be difficult to discuss workplace politics, much less to ask for help in developing political savvy. Even if you work in such an organization, there's still hope. In this section we provide simple ideas and exercises to help you accentuate skills, behaviors, and qualities that are vital to being effective in political environments.

Mingle Strategically

The ability to build strategic relationships and garner their support is important for the success of any leader. When it comes to building political savvy, however, it is essential.

> *"Connect with the right persons in your organization. On the job, your association and connection with the influencers gives you a voice where you might not have one otherwise."*

The easiest way to get started is to look at your current network. When you hear the word *networking*, you may think of handing out business cards, going to a networking or professional event, or even schmoozing. Networking goes far beyond that.

Think of networking as a way to build and enhance a support group of diverse people.

Leaders who possess a strong networking ability build cooperative, beneficial relationships with their colleagues. Networking comes easily to some people, while for others it feels like a political move. If you are among the latter, consider changing your thinking. In other words, think of networking as a way to build and enhance a support group of diverse people. If that doesn't sell the idea, think of the social capital you build by networking as a critical factor to your success and that of your team.

Exercise

Use the worksheet on page 14 to map your network. Write your name inside the oval. Then think of the people in your network, including those you would like to get to know because of their influence, power, reputation, or ability to get or dole out resources. Put the names of those you have strong or close connections with closer to your oval than those you have weak or distant connections with. Look for patterns in your connections. Also look to see whether those you have close connections with are in some way connected to those you have distant connections with, and consider whether you can get to know the latter through the former.

Your network probably includes peers and other people over whom you have no direct authority. To lead in contemporary organizations, you need to develop the ability to influence others in order to accomplish your organization's work. While this may not be new to you, the recognition that you already know how to negotiate and manage conflict among your peer networks is a step to building your political savvy. Remember that politics is not a zero-sum game; being politically savvy does not mean that someone else has to lose for you to win.

Don't forget to mingle with your boss and higher-ups. Managing up or keeping your boss and higher-ups informed is a politically savvy way to be successful in the workplace. If you think

Mapping My Network

your boss is too busy to hear about what you are doing, consider the following advice from a manager who participated in a research study that focused on organizational politics and political savvy:

> *"Manage upward. I was consistently advised by my senior VP to ensure that my project deliverables were clearly positioned and visible to the senior leadership team. She was right. Soon after the project concluded, I was promoted to another position in the organization, and I was able to bring my team along with me."*

What to Do

- ✔ Keep your boss informed by providing the information he or she needs.

- ✔ Be proactive in telling your boss what is going on, where struggles are, where things are going well. With this information, your boss won't be blindsided, and trust, rapport, and relationships can build.

- ✔ Identify people in your organization who are already politically savvy. Notice whom they network with and how they behave and carry themselves. Such observation and modeling can be very helpful in building your own savvy.

- ✔ Look for a mentor or coach to help you build your network. Think of this opportunity in terms of your current leadership role and your longer-term career goals. Being politically savvy can benefit both.

- ✔ Tell those you are close to (such as trusted peers or direct reports) about your intent to enhance your political savvy. Ask them to help you understand how you come across in social interactions, and whether you are coming across in a positive and effective manner. Ask them to buy in to your development, and do the same for them if they want you to. Such feedback is crucial to the successful development of the politically savvy leader.

Don't spend so much time managing up that you forget to develop and manage your direct reports. CCL research has discovered that some leaders' careers are likely to derail because their quest for visibility has blinded them to conflict within their teams. Being able to manage conflict is a necessary competency for the politically savvy leader. Mingling with a well-rounded network of people will help you balance the time necessary to manage conflict and negotiate for your teams.

Read the Situation

Building political savvy involves observation and gathering information. Consider this story of a manager who was able to read the situation and prepare herself to achieve her goal.

Sam was worried about her upcoming meeting with her boss and the CFO. The CFO had a reputation for being dictatorial and overly protective of his group and his own ideas. Sam had some bad news to share about a project that was already over budget, and the CFO's staff was hindering progress. Sam did her homework before the meeting. She checked around with others to learn how to influence the CFO. She gathered data showing how the project could be completed ahead of time with a little more investment and support from the financial office. Preparing for this meeting paid off in the end. Sam got her request.

Politically savvy managers tend to be perceptive observers of others and of social situations. This kind of social astuteness involves observation, self-awareness, and the ability to adapt and tailor behavior to different environmental conditions.

Exercise

Pay attention to the nonverbal behaviors of those around you. In your next meeting, try to get a sense of how people are really feeling, in addition to what they are saying. Many times, it's not the actual words that matter, but the feelings behind those words. People can pay more attention to nonverbal behaviors (such as gestures, postures, tone of voice, eye contact, and facial expressions) than words, particularly if the words are in direct contrast to the actions. Are people open to you and what you are saying (leaning toward you, with their arms uncrossed, making eye contact) or closed to you (pulling back away from you, crossing their arms or legs)? Paying attention to the nonverbal cues in the room can help you read the situation and understand how people are really feeling.

What to Do

- ✔ Practice active listening (pay attention, hold judgment, reflect, clarify, summarize, and share). You must be able to hear others in order to understand them.

- ✔ Think about how others must be feeling at the moment, what is happening to them, and what circumstances are bringing them to you.

- ✔ Pay attention to what others' body language is saying about the way they are feeling.

✔ Pay attention to your feelings and reactions. In other words, be in the moment. If in doubt, ask trusted colleagues who shared the same experience what they thought and experienced. Look beyond your own ideas, needs, and agendas, and consider other people's situations, priorities, and needs.

✔ Consider what you can give people, understand how and why your request may have a negative effect on others, and find a way to appeal to the common good.

✔ Think about areas that you perceive as your strengths and weaknesses. Ask for feedback from others (your boss, superiors, peers, direct reports, and customers, for example) about how they perceive you in those same areas. It can be a source of insight about whether your perceptions agree with those of others. It can also alert you to blind spots (areas where you think you have strengths but others see weaknesses) and hidden talents (areas where you think you have weaknesses but others see strengths).

 Reading the situation can take time. To really read the situation, you have to pay attention to what is going on around you. Listening is important, but don't spend so much time listening that you go into paralysis. Overexamination can lead to action avoidance if you're not careful.

Determine the Appropriate Behavior Before Acting

Count to 10, think twice before speaking, choose your battles—how many times have you heard or said one of these? Chances are there have been a lot. Impulse control is important, and it can also help you avoid a mistake like sharing an idea prematurely, shooting down another person's idea, telling an inappropriate joke, or using humor at the wrong time.

> *"Don't always say what is on your mind. I learned that the hard way, through experience in a meeting. My superior asked me for feedback and candor, so I gave him that. I told him I thought he was wrong and his dogmatic style was holding us back. I can think of at least three times that he has used it against me. My advice is to remember this: there are times to speak your mind and times to keep quiet."*

Direct reports characterize managers who lack impulse control as hostile, aggressive, and intolerant—especially when things don't go their way. Do you tend to remain calm in a crisis and when recovering from mistakes, or do you let your anger escalate and lead you down a path where you lose composure?

Clearly, the ability to resist or regulate impulsive behavior is a key factor in building political influence and putting your colleagues at ease. Improving impulse control is not impossible, but it can be difficult without help.

To lead in contemporary organizations, you need to develop the ability to influence others in order to accomplish your organization's work.

Exercise

Be constructive, not destructive, in handling disagreements or influencing others. Take a step back, gain perspective, and write down what you think would happen if you behave a certain way. Think about what others would think of you if you went with one action versus another. Also, write down what you think others are thinking or feeling in the situation. In other words, what is their perspective? Understanding their perspective can help you figure out what you should do in the situation. You may even want to go so far as to ask others what they are thinking or feeling to help you gain more perspective.

What to Do

✔ Consider working with a coach who can help you identify your hot buttons—issues that cause you to feel strong emotions—and ways to more effectively respond to them.

✔ If, after an honest assessment, you recognize that you tend to have trouble handling your emotions in difficult situations, consider attending an anger management or conflict management workshop. Such a workshop can help you set boundaries and control triggers that lead to outbursts and get you into trouble. Look for workshops that include assessment, feedback, modeling of new skills, practice of new skills, and ongoing support (so you won't lapse back into your old ways).

✔ Take a personality assessment. The knowledge you gain may help you understand how your personality preferences influence your behavior in response to various situations and people. You can identify skills and behaviors that contribute to your political savvy and see what you are doing that prevents or undermines your effectiveness at work.

Be careful that you don't overcorrect. Conflict is important for deeper thinking, results, and change. Try not to avoid or smooth over conflict for the sake of harmony and your personal gain. Being constructive in your dealings with others can help you resolve differences and overcome challenges that are inherent in dealing with people and getting work accomplished. There are competing interests, goals, and emotions in every situation. Politically savvy leaders work through these differences to come up with a win-win outcome.

Leave Them with a Good Impression

What kind of impression do you make on others? Do they consider you trustworthy?

"One of my colleagues had his career progression permanently derailed because he could not get others to trust him. His boss and others commented that he did not exhibit confidence in himself and, therefore, he could not influence and persuade others."

Whether or not you consider yourself politically savvy, you may have thought of workplace politics as manipulation. When asked if you want to manipulate your colleagues to get the much-needed funds for a top-priority project, you're likely to say no. But when asked if you could influence them in some way to get the funds, you probably would say yes. Manipulation is one form of influence that can alienate your colleagues even if it is considered a justifiable means to an end. Politically astute managers struggle in these situations, but they have learned that being authentic—honest, sincere, trustworthy, and genuine—inspires others to trust and have confidence in them.

Exercise

Record a video of yourself talking with a colleague, perhaps role-playing a difficult situation or a coaching situation. Afterward, watch the video with your colleague and others whom you trust, and comment on how you are coming across. Are you genuine in your actions? In other words, "does your audio match your video?" Take time to look at your behaviors on the video and ask how your behaviors and words make an impact on those who are observing.

What to Do

✔ Ask friends, coworkers, advisors, mentors, or coaches you trust to give you honest feedback on their perception of your style of influence. Are you able to exert influence in a manner that does not appear or feel manipulative, insincere, or backhanded?

✔ Pay attention to your nonverbal behaviors (your eye contact, your gestures). Keep eye contact; don't look at your watch or stare out the window when you are supposed to be listening. Make sure that your actions and words are in alignment.

✔ Keep people's confidences and avoid gossiping.

✔ Follow through on your promises. Sometimes this can be as simple as paying attention so that you do not overcommit.

✔ Make appeals based on logic, emotion, or a sense of cooperation as the situation dictates. Be agile in using all three; don't always depend on the same one.

✔ Role-play a situation in which you would need to influence someone who is considered difficult. Have someone else observe how well you employ and show your political savvy.

Don't try too hard to impress. It's easy to make promises when you're trying to impress others, but don't make promises you can't keep. It's also easy for people to spot insincerity. CCL's research has shown that failure to follow through on promises can result in career derailment. Managers who don't follow through can be perceived as betraying trust and intentionally saying things for their own advantage. Other CCL research relating to C-level executives has shown that character strengths, particularly integrity, are important to job performance. Integrity can be vitally important to your success as a manager.

Conclusion

There are many things that politics is not. Politics is not good or bad; it's a neutral and natural part of everyday life in organizations. Politics is not a zero-sum game; politically savvy individuals can use their influence in an effective, authentic manner so that all parties involved get something positive out of the experience. Politics is not about being false or inauthentic; instead, political savvy is about understanding how to use your skills, behaviors, and qualities to be effective, and sincerity is vital. Use the ideas and exercises in this guidebook to become a more politically savvy leader, and build your capacity to lead effectively in your organization.

Suggested Readings

Ferris, G. R., Davidson, S. L., & Perrewé, P. L. (2010). *Political skill at work: Impact on work effectiveness.* Boston, MA: Nicholas Brealey Publishing.

Grayson, C., & Baldwin, D. (2007). *Leadership networking: Connect, collaborate, create.* Greensboro, NC: Center for Creative Leadership.

Hernez-Broome, G., McLaughlin, C., & Trovas, S. (2006). *Selling yourself without selling out: A leader's guide to ethical self-promotion.* Greensboro, NC: Center for Creative Leadership.

Scharlatt, H. (2008). *Selling your ideas to your organization.* Greensboro, NC: Center for Creative Leadership.

Scharlatt, H., & Smith, R. (2011). *Influence: Gaining commitment, getting results* (2nd ed.). Greensboro, NC: Center for Creative Leadership.

Sharpe, D., & Johnson, E. (2002). *Managing conflict with your boss.* Greensboro, NC: Center for Creative Leadership.

Background

Since 1970, the Center for Creative Leadership has recognized the importance of influence skills in its research on learning from experience and in classroom discussions during leadership development programs. The Women's Leadership Program, for example, has long contained a segment focusing on influencing skills and organizational politics. First-level managers in CCL's Maximizing Your Leadership Potential program consistently speak of the difficulty of being in their first managerial jobs and having to influence those who used to be peers but are now direct reports, as well as having to influence their current peers, over whom they have no formal authority.

Yet we note that managers in our programs continue to struggle with the idea that political savvy may be an important component of leadership. They find it difficult to figure out how to appropriately incorporate effective leadership skills in inherently political environments. We decided to design a study that would examine the relationship of political savvy to effectiveness at work. Much of the work in the academic field has found a positive relationship between political skill and positive outcomes such as better job or team performance. Our own research shows that those who are politically savvy have better career prospects and trajectories, as they are seen as more promotable and less likely to show signs of career derailment (that is, being demoted, fired, or otherwise thrown off their intended career track).

Some may wonder whether there are gender differences in political savvy. In our research, we found no meaningful gender differences in the way men and women rate their own political savvy. We also found that the positive relationship between political savvy and performance was the same for men and women.

Key Point Summary

Organizational politics is neither good nor bad. Once you accept that politics is a natural part of everyday life in the workplace, you can build your capacity to lead effectively. You can be regarded as someone with effective political savvy, one who can influence and persuade others in a sincere, authentic manner.

One way to develop political savvy is to mingle strategically. The ability to build strategic relationships and garner their support is essential. Leaders who possess a strong networking ability build cooperative, beneficial relationships with their colleagues.

Building political savvy also involves the ability to read the situation. Politically savvy managers tend to be perceptive observers of others and of social situations. This kind of social astuteness involves observation, self-awareness, and the ability to adapt and tailor behavior to different environmental conditions.

It's important to determine the appropriate behavior before acting. Impulse control is necessary when you're in conflict, and it can also help you avoid a mistake like sharing an idea prematurely, shooting down another person's idea, telling an inappropriate joke, or using humor at the wrong time. The ability to resist or regulate impulsive behavior is a key factor in building political influence and putting your colleagues at ease.

Finally, leave people with a good impression. Avoid being manipulative. Being authentic—honest, sincere, trustworthy, and genuine—inspires others to trust and have confidence in you.

There are many things that politics is not. Politics is not good or bad; it's neutral and natural. Politics is not a zero-sum game; politically savvy individuals can use their influence in an effective, authentic manner so that all parties involved get something positive out of the experience. Politics is not about being false; instead, political savvy is about using your skills, behaviors, and qualities to be effective, and sincerity is vital.

Ordering Information

TO GET MORE INFORMATION, TO ORDER OTHER IDEAS INTO ACTION GUIDEBOOKS, OR TO FIND OUT ABOUT BULK-ORDER DISCOUNTS, PLEASE CONTACT US BY PHONE AT 336-545-2810 OR VISIT OUR ONLINE BOOKSTORE AT WWW.CCL.ORG/GUIDEBOOKS.